MznLnx

Missing Links Exam Preps

Exam Prep for

Beginning Algebra

Martin-Gay, 4th Edition

The MznLnx Exam Prep is your link from the texbook and lecture to your exams.
The MznLnx Exam Preps are unauthorized and comprehensive reviews of your textbooks.

All material provided by MznLnx and Rico Publications (c) 2010
Textbook publishers and textbook authors do not particpate in or contribute to these reviews.

MznLnx

Rico
Publications

Exam Prep for Beginning Algebra
4th Edition
Martin-Gay

Publisher: Raymond Houge
Assistant Editor: Michael Rouger
Text and Cover Designer: Lisa Buckner
Marketing Manager: Sara Swagger
Project Manager, Editorial Production: Jerry Emerson
Art Director: Vernon Lowerui

Product Manager: Dave Mason
Editorial Assitant: Rachel Guzmanji
Pedagogy: Debra Long
Cover Image: Jim Reed/Getty Images
Text and Cover Printer: City Printing, Inc.
Compositor: Media Mix, Inc.

(c) 2010 Rico Publications
ALL RIGHTS RESERVED. No part of this work covered by the copyright may be reproduced or used in any form or by an means--graphic, electronic, or mechanical, including photocopying, recording, taping, Web distribution, information storage, and retrieval systems, or in any other manner--without the written permission of the publisher.

Printed in the United States
ISBN:

For more information about our products, contact us at:
Dave.Mason@RicoPublications.com

For permission to use material from this text or product, submit a request online to:
Dave.Mason@RicoPublications.com

Contents

CHAPTER 1
REVIEW OF REAL NUMBERS   1

CHAPTER 2
EQUALITIES, AND PROBLEM SOLVING   9

CHAPTER 3
GRAPHING   13

CHAPTER 4
SOLVING SYSTEMS OF LINEAR EQUATIONS AND INEQUALITIES   16

CHAPTER 5
EXPONENTS AND POLYNOMIALS   19

CHAPTER 6
FACTORING POLYNOMIALS   24

CHAPTER 7
RATIONAL EXPRESSIONS   32

CHAPTER 8
ROOTS AND RADICALS   38

CHAPTER 9
SOLVING QUADRATIC EQUATIONS   44

ANSWER KEY   52

TO THE STUDENT

COMPREHENSIVE

The *MznLnx* Exam Prep series is designed to help you pass your exams. Editors at MznLnx review your textbooks and then prepare these practice exams to help you master the textbook material. Unlike study guides, workbooks, and practice tests provided by the texbook publisher and textbook authors, *MznLnx* gives you **all** of the material in each chapter in exam form, not just samples, so you can be sure to nail your exam.

MECHANICAL

The MznLnx Exam Prep series creates exams that will help you learn the subject matter as well as test you on your understanding. Each question is designed to help you master the concept. Just working through the exams, you gain an understanding of the subject--its a simple mechanical process that produces success.

INTEGRATED STUDY GUIDE AND REVIEW

MznLnx is not just a set of exams designed to test you, its also a comprehensive review of the subject content. Each exam question is also a review of the concept, making sure that you will get the answer correct without having to go to other sources of material. You learn as you go! Its the easiest way to pass an exam.

HUMOR

Studying can be tedious and dry. MznLnx's instructional design includes moderate humor within the exam questions on occassion, to break the tedium and revitalize the brain

Chapter 1. REVIEW OF REAL NUMBERS

1. A _____ is a symbol that stands for a value that may vary; the term usually occurs in opposition to constant, which is a symbol for a non-varying value, i.e. completely fixed or fixed in the context of use. The concepts of constants and variables are fundamental to all modern mathematics, science, engineering, and computer programming.

Much of the basic theory for which we use variables today, such as school geometry and algebra, was developed thousands of years ago, but the use of symbolic formulae and variables is only several hundreds of years old.

   a. -equivalence
   b. -module
   c. 2-bridge knot
   d. Variable

2. In mathematics, _____ of order k of functions is an equivalence relation, corresponding to having the same value at a point P and also the same derivatives there, up to order k. The equivalence classes are generally called jets. The point of osculation is also called the double cusp.
   a. Hessian matrix
   b. Laplace operator
   c. Contact
   d. Jacobian

3. In geometry, a _____ is a straight curve. When geometry is used to model the real world, lines are used to represent straight objects with negligible width and height. Lines are an idealisation of such objects and have no width or height at all and are usually considered to be infinitely long.
   a. -equivalence
   b. 2-bridge knot
   c. -module
   d. Line

4. In mathematics, an _____ is a statement about the relative size or order of two objects, or about whether they are the same or not

   - The notation a < b means that a is less than b.
   - The notation a > b means that a is greater than b.
   - The notation a ≠ b means that a is not equal to b, but does not say that one is bigger than the other or even that they can be compared in size.

In all these cases, a is not equal to b, hence, '_____'.

Chapter 1. REVIEW OF REAL NUMBERS

These relations are known as strict _____

- The notation a ≤ b means that a is less than or equal to b (or, equivalently, not greater than b);
- The notation a ≥ b means that a is greater than or equal to b (or, equivalently, not smaller than b);

An additional use of the notation is to show that one quantity is much greater than another, normally by several orders of magnitude.

- The notation a ≪ b means that a is much less than b.
- The notation a ≫ b means that a is much greater than b.

If the sense of the _____ is the same for all values of the variables for which its members are defined, then the _____ is called an 'absolute' or 'unconditional' _____. If the sense of an _____ holds only for certain values of the variables involved, but is reversed or destroyed for other values of the variables, it is called a conditional _____.

One can apply the same algebraic operations to inequalities as one would apply for solving equalities. For example, to find x for the _____ 10x > 20 one would divide 20 by 10 to obtain x > 2.

a. Abelian P-root group
b. ADE classification
c. AKS primality test
d. Inequality

5. The _____ are natural numbers including 0 ' href='/wiki/0_(number)'>0, 1, 2, 3, ...) and their negatives (0, −1, −2, −3, ...). They are numbers that can be written without a fractional or decimal component, and fall within the set {...
a. Integers
b. Abelian P-root group
c. ADE classification
d. AKS primality test

6. In mathematics, a _____ is any number that can be expressed in the form

$$\frac{a}{b}, a, b \in \mathbb{Z}, b \neq 0$$

which says 'a divided by b, given that a and b are integers and b does not equal zero'. Since the denominator b may be equal to 1, every integer is a _____. The set of all rational numbers is denoted $\mathbb{Q}$ (for quotient.)

a. Number system
b. Ratio
c. Rational number
d. -equivalence

7. In group theory, a branch of mathematics, the term _____ is used in two closely related senses:

- the _____ of a group is its cardinality, i.e. the number of its elements;
- the _____, sometimes period, of an element a of a group is the smallest positive integer m such that a^m = e (where e denotes the identity element of the group, and a^m denotes the product of m copies of a.) If no such m exists, we say that a has infinite _____. All elements of finite groups have finite _____.

We denote the _____ of a group G by ord(G) or $|G|$ and the _____ of an element a by ord(a) or $|a|$.

Example. The symmetric group S_3 has the following multiplication table.

This group has six elements, so ord(S_3) = 6.

a. Order
b. Index calculus algorithm
c. Artin group
d. Outer automorphism group

8. In mathematics, the _____ of a real number is its numerical value without regard to its sign. So, for example, 3 is the _____ of both 3 and −3.

The _____ of a number a is denoted by $|a|$.

a. AKS primality test
b. Abelian P-root group
c. ADE classification
d. Absolute value

9. _____ is the mathematical process of putting things together. The plus sign '+' means that numbers are added together. For example, in the picture on the right, there are 3 + 2 apples--meaning three apples and two other apples--which is the same as five apples, since 3 + 2 = 5.

a. ADE classification
b. Abelian P-root group
c. AKS primality test
d. Addition

10. _____ is one of the four basic arithmetic operations; it is the inverse of addition, meaning that if we start with any number and add any number and then subtract the same number we added, we return to the number we started with. _____ is denoted by a minus sign in infix notation.

The traditional names for the parts of the formula

$$c - b = a$$

are minuend (c) − subtrahend (b) = difference (a.)

a. -module
b. -equivalence
c. 2-bridge knot
d. Subtraction

11. In mathematics, the complex numbers are an extension of the real numbers obtained by adjoining an imaginary unit, denoted i, which satisfies:

$$i^2 = -1.$$

Every _____ can be written in the form a + bi, where a and b are real numbers called the real part and the imaginary part of the _____, respectively.

Complex numbers are a field, and thus have addition, subtraction, multiplication, and division operations. These operations extend the corresponding operations on real numbers, although with a number of additional elegant and useful properties, e.g., negative real numbers can be obtained by squaring complex (imaginary) numbers.

a. -equivalence
b. -module
c. 2-bridge knot
d. Complex number

Chapter 1. REVIEW OF REAL NUMBERS

12. A _____ is a three-dimensional solid object bounded by six square faces, facets or sides, with three meeting at each vertex. The _____ can also be called a regular hexahedron and is one of the five Platonic solids. It is a special kind of square prism, of rectangular parallelepiped and of trigonal trapezohedron.
    a. -equivalence
    b. 2-bridge knot
    c. -module
    d. Cube

13. In mathematics, the word _____ is a term for any well-formed combination of mathematical symbols. For example,

    $x^2 + 3x - 4$

    is an _____, while

    $)x) / 0$

    is not, because the parentheses are not balanced and division by zero is undefined.

    Being an _____ is a syntactic concept - the meaning of the variables is irrelevant, but different fields have different notions of validity.â€¢See formal language for how expressions are constructed, and formal semantics for meaning.

    a. Orthogonal
    b. Unit ring
    c. Expression
    d. Arity

14. In algebra and computer programming, when a number or expression is both preceded and followed by an operator such as minus or times, a rule is needed to specify which operator should be applied first; this rule is known as a _____, or more informally order of operation. From the earliest use of mathematical notation, multiplication took precedence over addition, whichever side of a number it appeared on. Thus 3 + 4 × 5 = 5 × 4 + 3 = 23.
    a. Planar ternary ring
    b. Setoid
    c. Precedence rule
    d. Formal power series

15. In its simplest meaning in mathematics and logic, an _____ is an action or procedure which produces a new value from one or more input values. There are two common types of operations: unary and binary. Unary operations involve only one value, such as negation and trigonometric functions.

   a. ADE classification
   b. AKS primality test
   c. Abelian P-root group
   d. Operation

16. The _____ of a Lie algebra 𝒈 is a particular ideal of 𝒈.

Let 𝒈 be a Lie algebra. The _____ of 𝒈 is defined as the largest solvable ideal of 𝒈.

   a. Cyclically reduced word
   b. Class sum
   c. Garside element
   d. Radical

17. In mathematics, a _____ of a number x is any number which, when repeatedly multiplied by itself, eventually yields x:

$$r \times r \times \cdots \times r = x.$$

In terms of exponentiation, r is a _____ of x if

$$r^n = x$$

for some positive integer n. For example, 2 is a _____ of 16 since $2^4 = 2 \times 2 \times 2 \times 2 = 16$.

The number n is called the degree of the _____.

   a. Cubic function
   b. Rationalisation
   c. Difference of two squares
   d. Root

18. In mathematics, the _____ of a number n is the number that, when added to n, yields zero. The _____ of F is denoted −F.

For example, the _____ of 7 is −7, because 7 + (−7) = 0, and the _____ of −0.3 is 0.3, because −0.3 + 0.3 = 0.

a. Artinian ideal
b. Interior algebra
c. Additive inverse
d. Isomorphism class

19. In geometry and trigonometry, an _____ is the figure formed by two rays sharing a common endpoint, called the vertex of the _____ . The magnitude of the _____ is the 'amount of rotation' that separates the two rays, and can be measured by considering the length of circular arc swept out when one ray is rotated about the vertex to coincide with the other Where there is no possibility of confusion, the term '_____' is used interchangeably for both the geometric configuration itself and for its angular magnitude (which is simply a numerical quantity.)

a. ADE classification
b. Angle
c. AKS primality test
d. Abelian P-root group

20. In mathematics, especially in elementary arithmetic, _____ is an arithmetic operation which is the inverse of multiplication.

Specifically, if c times b equals a, written:

$$c \times b = a$$

where b is not zero, then a divided by b equals c, written:

$$\frac{a}{b} = c$$

For instance,

$$\frac{6}{3} = 2$$

since

$$2 \times 3 = 6.$$

In the above expression, a is called the dividend, b the divisor and c the quotient.

a. -module
b. -equivalence
c. Division
d. 2-bridge knot

21. In mathematics, there are several meanings of _____ depending on the subject.

A _____, usually denoted by ° (the _____ symbol), is a measurement of plane angle, representing $\frac{1}{360}$ of a full rotation. When that angle is with respect to a reference meridian, it indicates a location along a great circle of a sphere, such as Earth, Mars, or the celestial sphere.

a. Relation algebra
b. Symmetric difference
c. Median algebra
d. Degree

22. In mathematics, a _____ or reciprocal for a number x, denoted by $\frac{1}{x}$ or x^{-1}, is a number which when multiplied by x yields the multiplicative identity, 1. The _____ of x is also called the reciprocal of x. The _____ of a fraction $\frac{a}{b}$ is $\frac{b}{a}$.

a. 2-bridge knot
b. -module
c. -equivalence
d. Multiplicative inverse

Chapter 2. EQUALITIES, AND PROBLEM SOLVING

1. In mathematics and group theory, a _____ system for the action of a group G on a set X is a partition of X that is G-invariant. In terms of the associated equivalence relation on X, G-invariance means that

    x ≡ y implies gx ≡ gy

for all g in G and all x, y in X. The action of G on X determines a natural action of G on any _____ system for X.

Each element of the _____ system is called a _____.

   a. Block
   b. Symmetric group
   c. Frobenius group
   d. Parker vector

2. In mathematics, a _____ is a constant multiplicative factor of a certain object. For example, in the expression $9x^2$, the _____ of x^2 is 9.

The object can be such things as a variable, a vector, a function, etc.

   a. Vandermonde polynomial
   b. Constant term
   c. Tschirnhaus transformation
   d. Coefficient

3. In mathematics, the word _____ is a term for any well-formed combination of mathematical symbols. For example,

    $x^2 + 3x - 4$

is an _____, while

)x) / 0

is not, because the parentheses are not balanced and division by zero is undefined.

Being an _____ is a syntactic concept - the meaning of the variables is irrelevant, but different fields have different notions of validity.âSee formal language for how expressions are constructed, and formal semantics for meaning.

Chapter 2. EQUALITIES, AND PROBLEM SOLVING

   a. Expression
   b. Orthogonal
   c. Arity
   d. Unit ring

4. _____ is the mathematical process of putting things together. The plus sign '+' means that numbers are added together. For example, in the picture on the right, there are 3 + 2 apples--meaning three apples and two other apples--which is the same as five apples, since 3 + 2 = 5.
   a. ADE classification
   b. AKS primality test
   c. Abelian P-root group
   d. Addition

5. The _____ of a Lie algebra $\mathfrak{g}$ is a particular ideal of $\mathfrak{g}$.

Let $\mathfrak{g}$ be a Lie algebra. The _____ of $\mathfrak{g}$ is defined as the largest solvable ideal of $\mathfrak{g}$.

   a. Cyclically reduced word
   b. Garside element
   c. Radical
   d. Class sum

6. A _____ is a symbol that stands for a value that may vary; the term usually occurs in opposition to constant, which is a symbol for a non-varying value, i.e. completely fixed or fixed in the context of use. The concepts of constants and variables are fundamental to all modern mathematics, science, engineering, and computer programming.

Much of the basic theory for which we use variables today, such as school geometry and algebra, was developed thousands of years ago, but the use of symbolic formulae and variables is only several hundreds of years old.

   a. -module
   b. -equivalence
   c. 2-bridge knot
   d. Variable

7. In commutative algebra, the term _____ refers to several related functors on topological rings and modules. _____ is similar to localization, and together they are among the most basic tools in analysing commutative rings. Complete commutative rings have simpler structure than the general ones, in large part, due to Hensel's lemma.

a. Local analysis
b. Localization of a category
c. Localized
d. Completion

8. The _____ are natural numbers including 0 ' href='/wiki/0_(number)'>0, 1, 2, 3, ...) and their negatives (0, −1, −2, −3, ...). They are numbers that can be written without a fractional or decimal component, and fall within the set {...
a. Abelian P-root group
b. AKS primality test
c. ADE classification
d. Integers

9. In mathematics, and more specifically set theory, the _____ is the unique set having no (zero) members. Some axiomatic set theories assure that the _____ exists by including an axiom of _____; in other theories, its existence can be deduced. Many possible properties of sets are trivially true for the _____.
a. AKS primality test
b. ADE classification
c. Abelian P-root group
d. Empty set

10. In mathematics, the term _____ is used to describe an algebraic structures which in some sense cannot be divided by a smaller structure of the same type. Put another way, an algebraic structure is _____ if the kernel of every homomorphism is either the whole structure or a single element. Some examples are:

- A group is called a _____ group if it does not contain a non-trivial proper normal subgroup.
- A ring is called a _____ ring if it does not contain a non-trivial two sided ideal.
- A module is called a _____ module if does not contain a non-trivial submodule.
- An algebra is called a _____ algebra if does not contain a non-trivial two sided ideal.

The general pattern is that the structure admits no non-trivial congruence relations.

a. Commutativity
b. Simple
c. Linear combinations
d. Polarization identity

Chapter 2. EQUALITIES, AND PROBLEM SOLVING

11. In mathematics, an _____ is a statement about the relative size or order of two objects, or about whether they are the same or not

- The notation a < b means that a is less than b.
- The notation a > b means that a is greater than b.
- The notation a ≠ b means that a is not equal to b, but does not say that one is bigger than the other or even that they can be compared in size.

In all these cases, a is not equal to b, hence, '_____'.

These relations are known as strict _____

- The notation a ≤ b means that a is less than or equal to b (or, equivalently, not greater than b);
- The notation a ≥ b means that a is greater than or equal to b (or, equivalently, not smaller than b);

An additional use of the notation is to show that one quantity is much greater than another, normally by several orders of magnitude.

- The notation a ≪ b means that a is much less than b.
- The notation a ≫ b means that a is much greater than b.

If the sense of the _____ is the same for all values of the variables for which its members are defined, then the _____ is called an 'absolute' or 'unconditional' _____. If the sense of an _____ holds only for certain values of the variables involved, but is reversed or destroyed for other values of the variables, it is called a conditional _____.

One can apply the same algebraic operations to inequalities as one would apply for solving equalities. For example, to find x for the _____ 10x > 20 one would divide 20 by 10 to obtain x > 2.

a. ADE classification
b. AKS primality test
c. Abelian P-root group
d. Inequality

Chapter 3. GRAPHING

1. In mathematics, a (B, N) _____ is a structure on groups of Lie type that allows one to give uniform proofs of many results, instead of giving a large number of case-by-case proofs. Roughly speaking, it shows that all such groups are similar to the general linear group over a field. They were invented by the mathematician Jacques Tits, and are also sometimes known as Tits systems.

   a. Group action
   b. Group representations
   c. Pair
   d. Rank of a group

2. A _____ is a symbol that stands for a value that may vary; the term usually occurs in opposition to constant, which is a symbol for a non-varying value, i.e. completely fixed or fixed in the context of use. The concepts of constants and variables are fundamental to all modern mathematics, science, engineering, and computer programming.

   Much of the basic theory for which we use variables today, such as school geometry and algebra, was developed thousands of years ago, but the use of symbolic formulae and variables is only several hundreds of years old.

   a. -equivalence
   b. 2-bridge knot
   c. -module
   d. Variable

3. In mathematics, the complex numbers are an extension of the real numbers obtained by adjoining an imaginary unit, denoted i, which satisfies:

   $$i^2 = -1.$$

   Every _____ can be written in the form a + bi, where a and b are real numbers called the real part and the imaginary part of the _____, respectively.

   Complex numbers are a field, and thus have addition, subtraction, multiplication, and division operations. These operations extend the corresponding operations on real numbers, although with a number of additional elegant and useful properties, e.g., negative real numbers can be obtained by squaring complex (imaginary) numbers.

   a. 2-bridge knot
   b. Complex number
   c. -equivalence
   d. -module

4. In geometry, a _____ is a straight curve. When geometry is used to model the real world, lines are used to represent straight objects with negligible width and height. Lines are an idealisation of such objects and have no width or height at all and are usually considered to be infinitely long.
   a. -equivalence
   b. 2-bridge knot
   c. -module
   d. Line

5. In mathematics, there are several meanings of _____ depending on the subject.

A _____, usually denoted by ° (the _____ symbol), is a measurement of plane angle, representing $\frac{1}{360}$ of a full rotation. When that angle is with respect to a reference meridian, it indicates a location along a great circle of a sphere, such as Earth, Mars, or the celestial sphere.

   a. Degree
   b. Median algebra
   c. Relation algebra
   d. Symmetric difference

6. In geometry, two lines or planes (or a line and a plane), are considered _____ to each other if they form congruent adjacent angles (an L-shape.) The term may be used as a noun or adjective. Thus, referring to Figure 1, the line AB is the _____ to CD through the point B. Note that by definition, a line is infinitely long, and strictly speaking AB and CD in this example represent line segments of two infinitely long lines.
   a. 2-bridge knot
   b. -equivalence
   c. Perpendicular
   d. -module

7. In mathematics, the _____ of a number n is the number that, when added to n, yields zero. The _____ of F is denoted −F.

For example, the _____ of 7 is −7, because 7 + (−7) = 0, and the _____ of −0.3 is 0.3, because −0.3 + 0.3 = 0.

a. Additive inverse
b. Isomorphism class
c. Artinian ideal
d. Interior algebra

8. In mathematics, especially in the area of abstract algebra known as ring theory, a _____ is a ring with 0 ≠ 1 such that ab = 0 implies that either a = 0 or b = 0 (the zero-product property.) That is, it is a nontrivial ring without left or right zero divisors. A commutative _____ is called an integral _____.
a. Coherent ring
b. Partially-ordered ring
c. Subring
d. Domain

Chapter 4. SOLVING SYSTEMS OF LINEAR EQUATIONS AND INEQUALITIES

1. The _____ of a Lie algebra $\mathfrak{g}$ is a particular ideal of $\mathfrak{g}$.

Let $\mathfrak{g}$ be a Lie algebra. The _____ of $\mathfrak{g}$ is defined as the largest solvable ideal of $\mathfrak{g}$.

   a. Cyclically reduced word
   b. Class sum
   c. Garside element
   d. Radical

2. An _____ is an equation in a system of simultaneous equations which cannot be derived algebraically from the other equations.

   a. Eigendecomposition
   b. Orthogonalization
   c. Elementary matrix
   d. Independent equation

3. _____ is the mathematical process of putting things together. The plus sign '+' means that numbers are added together. For example, in the picture on the right, there are 3 + 2 apples--meaning three apples and two other apples--which is the same as five apples, since 3 + 2 = 5.

   a. AKS primality test
   b. ADE classification
   c. Abelian P-root group
   d. Addition

4. A _____ is a symbol that stands for a value that may vary; the term usually occurs in opposition to constant, which is a symbol for a non-varying value, i.e. completely fixed or fixed in the context of use. The concepts of constants and variables are fundamental to all modern mathematics, science, engineering, and computer programming.

Much of the basic theory for which we use variables today, such as school geometry and algebra, was developed thousands of years ago, but the use of symbolic formulae and variables is only several hundreds of years old.

   a. 2-bridge knot
   b. Variable
   c. -equivalence
   d. -module

5. If the space is two-dimensional, then a half-space is called a _____ A half-space in a one-dimensional space is called a ray.

Chapter 4. SOLVING SYSTEMS OF LINEAR EQUATIONS AND INEQUALITIES

A half-space may be specified by a linear inequality, derived from the linear equation that specifies the defining hyperplane.

a. -module
b. -equivalence
c. 2-bridge knot
d. Half-plane

6. In geometry, a _____ is a straight curve. When geometry is used to model the real world, lines are used to represent straight objects with negligible width and height. Lines are an idealisation of such objects and have no width or height at all and are usually considered to be infinitely long.

a. 2-bridge knot
b. -module
c. Line
d. -equivalence

7. In mathematics, a (B, N) _____ is a structure on groups of Lie type that allows one to give uniform proofs of many results, instead of giving a large number of case-by-case proofs. Roughly speaking, it shows that all such groups are similar to the general linear group over a field. They were invented by the mathematician Jacques Tits, and are also sometimes known as Tits systems.

a. Pair
b. Group representations
c. Group action
d. Rank of a group

8. In mathematics, an _____ is a statement about the relative size or order of two objects, or about whether they are the same or not

- The notation a < b means that a is less than b.
- The notation a > b means that a is greater than b.
- The notation a ≠ b means that a is not equal to b, but does not say that one is bigger than the other or even that they can be compared in size.

In all these cases, a is not equal to b, hence, '_____'.

Chapter 4. SOLVING SYSTEMS OF LINEAR EQUATIONS AND INEQUALITIES

These relations are known as strict _____

- The notation a ≤ b means that a is less than or equal to b (or, equivalently, not greater than b);
- The notation a ≥ b means that a is greater than or equal to b (or, equivalently, not smaller than b);

An additional use of the notation is to show that one quantity is much greater than another, normally by several orders of magnitude.

- The notation a ≪ b means that a is much less than b.
- The notation a ≫ b means that a is much greater than b.

If the sense of the _____ is the same for all values of the variables for which its members are defined, then the _____ is called an 'absolute' or 'unconditional' _____. If the sense of an _____ holds only for certain values of the variables involved, but is reversed or destroyed for other values of the variables, it is called a conditional _____.

One can apply the same algebraic operations to inequalities as one would apply for solving equalities. For example, to find x for the _____ 10x > 20 one would divide 20 by 10 to obtain x > 2.

a. Inequality
b. ADE classification
c. Abelian P-root group
d. AKS primality test

Chapter 5. EXPONENTS AND POLYNOMIALS

1. In mathematics, the word _____ is a term for any well-formed combination of mathematical symbols. For example,

   $x^2 + 3x - 4$

   is an _____, while

)x) / 0

   is not, because the parentheses are not balanced and division by zero is undefined.

   Being an _____ is a syntactic concept - the meaning of the variables is irrelevant, but different fields have different notions of validity.â€€See formal language for how expressions are constructed, and formal semantics for meaning.

   a. Orthogonal
   b. Unit ring
   c. Arity
   d. Expression

2. _____ is the mathematical process of putting things together. The plus sign '+' means that numbers are added together. For example, in the picture on the right, there are 3 + 2 apples--meaning three apples and two other apples--which is the same as five apples, since 3 + 2 = 5.
   a. AKS primality test
   b. Abelian P-root group
   c. ADE classification
   d. Addition

3. In mathematics, especially in elementary arithmetic, _____ is an arithmetic operation which is the inverse of multiplication.

   Specifically, if c times b equals a, written:

   $$c \times b = a$$

   where b is not zero, then a divided by b equals c, written:

   $$\frac{a}{b} = c$$

Chapter 5. EXPONENTS AND POLYNOMIALS

For instance,

$$\frac{6}{3} = 2$$

since

$$2 \times 3 = 6.$$

In the above expression, a is called the dividend, b the divisor and c the quotient.

a. 2-bridge knot
b. -module
c. -equivalence
d. Division

4. _____ is one of the four basic arithmetic operations; it is the inverse of addition, meaning that if we start with any number and add any number and then subtract the same number we added, we return to the number we started with. _____ is denoted by a minus sign in infix notation.

The traditional names for the parts of the formula

c − b = a

are minuend (c) − subtrahend (b) = difference (a.)

a. -equivalence
b. Subtraction
c. 2-bridge knot
d. -module

5. In mathematics, the complex numbers are an extension of the real numbers obtained by adjoining an imaginary unit, denoted i, which satisfies:

$$i^2 = -1.$$

Every _____ can be written in the form a + bi, where a and b are real numbers called the real part and the imaginary part of the _____, respectively.

Chapter 5. EXPONENTS AND POLYNOMIALS

Complex numbers are a field, and thus have addition, subtraction, multiplication, and division operations. These operations extend the corresponding operations on real numbers, although with a number of additional elegant and useful properties, e.g., negative real numbers can be obtained by squaring complex (imaginary) numbers.

a. 2-bridge knot
b. -equivalence
c. Complex number
d. -module

6. In elementary algebra, a _____ is a polynomial with two terms--the sum of two monomials--often bound by parenthesis or brackets when operated upon. It is the simplest kind of polynomial other than monomials.

- The _____ $a^2 - b^2$ can be factored as the product of two other binomials:

    $a^2 - b^2 = (a + b)(a - b.)$

    This is a special case of the more general formula:

    $$a^{n+1} - b^{n+1} = (a-b)\sum_{k=0}^{n} a^k b^{n-k}$$.

- The product of a pair of linear binomials (ax + b) and (cx + d) is:

    $(ax + b)(cx + d) = acx^2 + axd + bcx + bd$.

- A _____ raised to the nth power, represented as

    $(a + b)^n$

    can be expanded by means of the _____ theorem or, equivalently, using Pascal's triangle. Taking a simple example, the perfect square _____ $(p + q)^2$ can be found by squaring the :first digit, adding twice the product of the first and second digit and finally adding the square of the second digit, to give $p^2 + 2pq + q^2$.

a. Generalized arithmetic progression
b. Theory of equations
c. Content
d. Binomial

7. In mathematics, a _____ is a constant multiplicative factor of a certain object. For example, in the expression 9x^2, the _____ of x^2 is 9.

The object can be such things as a variable, a vector, a function, etc.

Chapter 5. EXPONENTS AND POLYNOMIALS

a. Vandermonde polynomial
b. Constant term
c. Tschirnhaus transformation
d. Coefficient

8. In mathematics, there are several meanings of _____ depending on the subject.

A _____, usually denoted by ° (the _____ symbol), is a measurement of plane angle, representing $\frac{1}{360}$ of a full rotation. When that angle is with respect to a reference meridian, it indicates a location along a great circle of a sphere, such as Earth, Mars, or the celestial sphere.

a. Median algebra
b. Symmetric difference
c. Relation algebra
d. Degree

9. In mathematics, the word _____ means two different things in the context of polynomials:

- The first meaning is a product of powers of variables, or formally any value obtained from 1 by finitely many multiplications by a variable. If only a single variable x is considered this means that any _____ is either 1 or a power x^n of x, with n a positive integer. If several variables are considered, say, x, y, z, then each can be given an exponent, so that any _____ is of the form $x^a y^b z^c$ with a,b,c nonnegative integers (taking note that any exponent 0 makes the corresponding factor equal to 1.)
- The second meaning of _____ includes monomials in the first sense, but also allows multiplication by any constant, so that $-7x^5$ and $(3-4i)x^4yz^{13}$ are also considered to be monomials (the second example assuming polynomials in x, y, z over the complex numbers are considered.)

With either definition, the set of monomials is a subset of all polynomials that is closed under multiplication.

Both uses of this notion can be found, and in many cases the distinction is simply ignored, see for instance examples for the first and second meaning, and an unclear definition. In informal discussions the distinction is seldom important, and tendency is towards the broader second meaning. When studying the structure of polynomials however, one often definitely needs a notion with the first meaning.

a. Diagonal form
b. Power sum symmetric polynomial
c. Monomial
d. Schur polynomials

Chapter 5. EXPONENTS AND POLYNOMIALS

10. In elementary algebra, a _____ is a polynomial consisting of three terms; in other words, a _____ is the sum of three monomials. It can be factored using simple steps.

In linguistics, a _____ is a fixed expression which is made from three words; e.g. 'lights, camera, action', 'signed, sealed, delivered'.

a. Trinomial
b. Finitary operation
c. Hall polynomials
d. Polynomial Diophantine equation

11. In mathematics, the _____ of a polynomial is the term of degree 0. For example, in the polynomial

$$X^3 + 2X + 3$$

over the variable X, the _____ is 3. Here, the _____ is given by a numeral, but it may also be specified by a letter that is a parameter rather than a variable, as in the polynomial

$$ax^2 + bx + c,$$

in the variable x, where a, b, and c are parameters so that c is the _____.

a. Characteristic polynomial
b. Quadratic function
c. Symmetric polynomial
d. Constant Term

12. The _____ are natural numbers including 0 ' href='/wiki/0_(number)'>0, 1, 2, 3, ...) and their negatives (0, −1, −2, −3, ...). They are numbers that can be written without a fractional or decimal component, and fall within the set {...

a. Abelian P-root group
b. ADE classification
c. Integers
d. AKS primality test

Chapter 6. FACTORING POLYNOMIALS

1. In mathematics, _____ (F_n) is the outer automorphism group of a free group on n generators. These groups play an important role in geometric group theory.

   _____ (F_n) acts geometrically on a cell complex known as outer space, which can be thought of as the Teichmüller space for a bouquet of circles.

   a. ADE classification
   b. Out
   c. Abelian P-root group
   d. AKS primality test

2. In elementary algebra, a _____ is a polynomial consisting of three terms; in other words, a _____ is the sum of three monomials. It can be factored using simple steps.

   In linguistics, a _____ is a fixed expression which is made from three words; e.g. 'lights, camera, action', 'signed, sealed, delivered'.

   a. Finitary operation
   b. Polynomial Diophantine equation
   c. Hall polynomials
   d. Trinomial

3. In elementary algebra, a _____ is a polynomial with two terms--the sum of two monomials--often bound by parenthesis or brackets when operated upon. It is the simplest kind of polynomial other than monomials.

   - The _____ $a^2 - b^2$ can be factored as the product of two other binomials:

     $a^2 - b^2 = (a + b)(a - b.)$

     This is a special case of the more general formula:

     $$a^{n+1} - b^{n+1} = (a - b) \sum_{k=0}^{n} a^k b^{n-k}$$

   - The product of a pair of linear binomials (ax + b) and (cx + d) is:

     $(ax + b)(cx + d) = acx^2 + axd + bcx + bd.$

   - A _____ raised to the nth power, represented as

     $(a + b)^n$

     can be expanded by means of the _____ theorem or, equivalently, using Pascal's triangle. Taking a simple example, the perfect square _____ $(p + q)^2$ can be found by squaring the :first digit, adding twice the product of the first and second digit and finally adding the square of the second digit, to give $p^2 + 2pq + q^2$.

a. Content
b. Generalized arithmetic progression
c. Theory of equations
d. Binomial

4. A _____ is a three-dimensional solid object bounded by six square faces, facets or sides, with three meeting at each vertex. The _____ can also be called a regular hexahedron and is one of the five Platonic solids. It is a special kind of square prism, of rectangular parallelepiped and of trigonal trapezohedron.

   a. 2-bridge knot
   b. -module
   c. -equivalence
   d. Cube

5. In mathematics, the _____ is when a number is squared and is then subtracted from another squared number. It refers to the identity

$$a^2 - b^2 = (a+b)(a-b)$$

from elementary algebra.

The proof is straightforward, starting from the RHS: apply the distributive law to get a sum of four terms, and set

$$ba - ab = 0$$

as an application of the commutative law.

   a. Cubic function
   b. Difference of two squares
   c. Pointwise product
   d. FOIL rule

6. _____ is a concept that permeates much of inferential statistics and descriptive statistics. More properly, it is 'the sum of the squared deviations'. Mathematically, it is an unscaled, or unadjusted measure of dispersion (also called variability.)

a. -equivalence
b. -module
c. 2-bridge knot
d. Sum of squares

7. In mathematics, the word _____ is a term for any well-formed combination of mathematical symbols. For example,

   $x^2 + 3x - 4$

is an _____, while

)x) / 0

is not, because the parentheses are not balanced and division by zero is undefined.

Being an _____ is a syntactic concept - the meaning of the variables is irrelevant, but different fields have different notions of validity.â€¢See formal language for how expressions are constructed, and formal semantics for meaning.

a. Arity
b. Orthogonal
c. Unit ring
d. Expression

8. In mathematics, a _____ is a polynomial equation of the second degree. The general form is

$$ax^2 + bx + c = 0$$

The quadratic coefficient a is the coefficient of x^2, the linear coefficient b is the coefficient of x, and c is the constant coefficient, also called the free term or constant term.

Quadratic equations are called quadratic because the variable in the leading term is squared.

a. Difference of two squares
b. Cubic function
c. Rationalisation
d. Quadratic equation

9. In elementary algebra, _____ is a technique for converting a quadratic polynomial of the form

Chapter 6. FACTORING POLYNOMIALS

$$ax^2 + bx + c$$

to the form

$$a(\cdots\cdots)^2 + \text{constant}.$$

The expression inside the parenthesis is of the form x − constant. Thus one converts $ax^2 + bx + c$ to

$$a(x - h)^2 + k$$

and one must find h and k.

_____ is used in

- solving quadratic equations,
- graphing quadratic functions,
- evaluating integrals in calculus,
- finding Laplace transforms.

In mathematics, _____ is considered a basic algebraic operation, and is often applied without remark in any computation involving quadratic polynomials.

There is a simple formula in elementary algebra for computing the square of a binomial:

$$(x + p)^2 = x^2 + 2px + p^2.$$

For example:

$$(x + 3)^2 = x^2 + 6x + 9 \qquad (p = 3)$$
$$(x - 5)^2 = x^2 - 10x + 25 \qquad (p = -5).$$

In any perfect square, the number p is always half the coefficient of x, and then the constant term is equal to p^2.

a. Content
b. Nested radical
c. Reduct
d. Completing the square

Chapter 6. FACTORING POLYNOMIALS

10. In mathematics, the complex numbers are an extension of the real numbers obtained by adjoining an imaginary unit, denoted i, which satisfies:

$$i^2 = -1.$$

Every _____ can be written in the form a + bi, where a and b are real numbers called the real part and the imaginary part of the _____, respectively.

Complex numbers are a field, and thus have addition, subtraction, multiplication, and division operations. These operations extend the corresponding operations on real numbers, although with a number of additional elegant and useful properties, e.g., negative real numbers can be obtained by squaring complex (imaginary) numbers.

a. -module
b. Complex number
c. -equivalence
d. 2-bridge knot

11. In algebra, the _____ is a theorem for finding out the factors of a polynomial (an expression in which the terms are only added, subtracted or multiplied, e.g. x^2 + 6x + 6.) It is a special case of the polynomial remainder theorem.

The _____ states that a polynomial f(x) has a factor x − k if and only if f(k) = 0.

a. Remez algorithm
b. Difference polynomial
c. Quadratic function
d. Factor theorem

12. The _____ of a Lie algebra $\mathfrak{g}$ is a particular ideal of $\mathfrak{g}$.

Let $\mathfrak{g}$ be a Lie algebra. The _____ of $\mathfrak{g}$ is defined as the largest solvable ideal of $\mathfrak{g}$.

a. Radical
b. Cyclically reduced word
c. Class sum
d. Garside element

13. A _____ is a symbol that stands for a value that may vary; the term usually occurs in opposition to constant, which is a symbol for a non-varying value, i.e. completely fixed or fixed in the context of use. The concepts of constants and variables are fundamental to all modern mathematics, science, engineering, and computer programming.

Chapter 6. FACTORING POLYNOMIALS

Much of the basic theory for which we use variables today, such as school geometry and algebra, was developed thousands of years ago, but the use of symbolic formulae and variables is only several hundreds of years old.

a. -equivalence
b. 2-bridge knot
c. -module
d. Variable

14. In mathematics, the _____ is a conic section, the intersection of a right circular conical surface and a plane parallel to a generating straight line of that surface. Given a point (the focus) and a line (the directrix) that lie in a plane, the locus of points in that plane that are equidistant to them is a _____.

A particular case arises when the plane is tangent to the conical surface of a circle.

a. -equivalence
b. -module
c. 2-bridge knot
d. Parabola

15. In abstract algebra, the _____ of a module is a measure of the module's 'size'. It is defined as the _____ of the longest ascending chain of submodules and is a generalization of the concept of dimension for vector spaces. The modules with finite _____ share many important properties with finite-dimensional vector spaces.
a. Morita equivalence
b. Finitely generated module
c. Supermodule
d. Length

16. In mathematics, a _____ of a number x is any number which, when repeatedly multiplied by itself, eventually yields x:

$$r \times r \times \cdots \times r = x.$$

In terms of exponentiation, r is a _____ of x if

$$r^n = x$$

for some positive integer n. For example, 2 is a _____ of 16 since $2^4 = 2 \times 2 \times 2 \times 2 = 16$.

The number n is called the degree of the _____.

a. Rationalisation
b. ROOT
c. Cubic function
d. Difference of two squares

17. In linear algebra, the _____ of an n-by-n square matrix A is defined to be the sum of the elements on the main diagonal (the diagonal from the upper left to the lower right) of A, i.e.,

$$\operatorname{tr}(A) = a_{11} + a_{22} + \cdots + a_{nn} = \sum_{i=1}^{n} a_{ii}$$

where a_{ij} represents the entry on the ith row and jth column of A. Equivalently, the _____ of a matrix is the sum of its eigenvalues, making it an invariant with respect to a change of basis. This characterization can be used to define the _____ for a linear operator in general.

Note that the _____ is only defined for a square matrix (i.e. n×n.)

a. Dot product
b. TRACE
c. Coefficient matrix
d. Defective matrix

18. A _____ is a triangle in which one angle is a right angle.

The side opposite the right angle is called the hypotenuse (side [BC] in the figure below.) In addition, the sides adjacent to the right angle are called legs or catheti (singular: cathetus.)

a. -module
b. -equivalence
c. Right triangle
d. 2-bridge knot

19. A _____ is one of the basic shapes of geometry: a polygon with three corners or vertices and three sides or edges which are line segments. A _____ with vertices A, B, and C is denoted ABC.

Chapter 6. FACTORING POLYNOMIALS

In Euclidean geometry any three non-collinear points determine a unique _____ and a unique plane (i.e. a two-dimensional Euclidean space.)

a. Triangle
b. -module
c. -equivalence
d. 2-bridge knot

20. In mathematics, the _____ of a vector space V is the cardinality (i.e. the number of vectors) of a basis of V. It is sometimes called Hamel _____ or algebraic _____ to distinguish it from other types of _____. All bases of a vector space have equal cardinality and so the _____ of a vector space is uniquely defined. The _____ of the vector space V over the field F can be written as $\dim_F(V)$ or as [V : F], read '_____ of V over F'.

a. Partial trace
b. Dimension
c. Dual basis
d. Cofactor

21. The _____ are natural numbers including 0 ' href='/wiki/0_(number)'>0, 1, 2, 3, ...) and their negatives (0, −1, −2, −3, ...). They are numbers that can be written without a fractional or decimal component, and fall within the set {...

a. ADE classification
b. AKS primality test
c. Abelian P-root group
d. Integers

Chapter 7. RATIONAL EXPRESSIONS

1. In mathematics, especially in elementary arithmetic, _____ is an arithmetic operation which is the inverse of multiplication.

Specifically, if c times b equals a, written:

$$c \times b = a$$

where b is not zero, then a divided by b equals c, written:

$$\frac{a}{b} = c$$

For instance,

$$\frac{6}{3} = 2$$

since

$$2 \times 3 = 6.$$

In the above expression, a is called the dividend, b the divisor and c the quotient.

   a. -module
   b. 2-bridge knot
   c. -equivalence
   d. Division

2. In mathematics, the word _____ is a term for any well-formed combination of mathematical symbols. For example,

    $x^2 + 3x - 4$

is an _____, while

)x) / 0

is not, because the parentheses are not balanced and division by zero is undefined.

Being an _____ is a syntactic concept - the meaning of the variables is irrelevant, but different fields have different notions of validity.â€See formal language for how expressions are constructed, and formal semantics for meaning.

Chapter 7. RATIONAL EXPRESSIONS

   a. Expression
   b. Orthogonal
   c. Unit ring
   d. Arity

3. In mathematics, the complex numbers are an extension of the real numbers obtained by adjoining an imaginary unit, denoted i, which satisfies:

$$i^2 = -1.$$

Every _____ can be written in the form a + bi, where a and b are real numbers called the real part and the imaginary part of the _____, respectively.

Complex numbers are a field, and thus have addition, subtraction, multiplication, and division operations. These operations extend the corresponding operations on real numbers, although with a number of additional elegant and useful properties, e.g., negative real numbers can be obtained by squaring complex (imaginary) numbers.

   a. -equivalence
   b. -module
   c. 2-bridge knot
   d. Complex number

4. In mathematics, there are several meanings of _____ depending on the subject.

A _____, usually denoted by ° (the _____ symbol), is a measurement of plane angle, representing $1/360$ of a full rotation. When that angle is with respect to a reference meridian, it indicates a location along a great circle of a sphere, such as Earth , Mars, or the celestial sphere.

   a. Relation algebra
   b. Degree
   c. Median algebra
   d. Symmetric difference

5. In mathematics, a _____ in a (unital) ring R is an invertible element of R, i.e. an element u such that there is a v in R with

uv = vu = 1_R, where 1_R is the multiplicative identity element.

Chapter 7. RATIONAL EXPRESSIONS

That is, u is an invertible element of the multiplicative monoid of R. If $0 \neq 1$ in the ring, then 0 is not a _____.

Unfortunately, the term _____ is also used to refer to the identity element 1_R of the ring, in expressions like ring with a _____ or _____ ring, and also e.g. '_____' matrix.

a. Ore extension
b. Ascending chain condition on principal ideals
c. Ore condition
d. Unit

6. _____ is the mathematical process of putting things together. The plus sign '+' means that numbers are added together. For example, in the picture on the right, there are 3 + 2 apples--meaning three apples and two other apples--which is the same as five apples, since 3 + 2 = 5.

a. ADE classification
b. AKS primality test
c. Abelian P-root group
d. Addition

7. _____ is one of the four basic arithmetic operations; it is the inverse of addition, meaning that if we start with any number and add any number and then subtract the same number we added, we return to the number we started with. _____ is denoted by a minus sign in infix notation.

The traditional names for the parts of the formula

    c − b = a

are minuend (c) − subtrahend (b) = difference (a.)

a. -module
b. 2-bridge knot
c. -equivalence
d. Subtraction

8. The _____ of a Lie algebra $\mathfrak{g}$ is a particular ideal of $\mathfrak{g}$.

Let $\mathfrak{g}$ be a Lie algebra. The _____ of $\mathfrak{g}$ is defined as the largest solvable ideal of $\mathfrak{g}$.

Chapter 7. RATIONAL EXPRESSIONS

a. Garside element
b. Radical
c. Cyclically reduced word
d. Class sum

9. A _____ is a symbol that stands for a value that may vary; the term usually occurs in opposition to constant, which is a symbol for a non-varying value, i.e. completely fixed or fixed in the context of use. The concepts of constants and variables are fundamental to all modern mathematics, science, engineering, and computer programming.

Much of the basic theory for which we use variables today, such as school geometry and algebra, was developed thousands of years ago, but the use of symbolic formulae and variables is only several hundreds of years old.

a. 2-bridge knot
b. -equivalence
c. -module
d. Variable

10. In mathematics, the _____ is a binary operation on two vectors in a three-dimensional Euclidean space that results in another vector which is perpendicular to the plane containing the two input vectors. The algebra defined by the _____ is neither commutative nor associative. It contrasts with the dot product which produces a scalar result.
    a. Row space
    b. Differential graded algebra
    c. Formal power series
    d. Cross product

11. A _____ is an expression which compares quantities relative to each other. The most common examples involve two quantities, but in theory any number of quantities can be compared. In mathematical terms, they are represented by separating each quantity with a colon, for example the _____ 2:3, which is read as the _____ 'two to three'.
    a. Ratio
    b. -equivalence
    c. Number system
    d. Rational number

12. In linear algebra, two n-by-n matrices A and B are called _____ if

$$B = P^{-1}AP$$

for some invertible n-by-n matrix P. _____ matrices represent the same linear transformation under two different bases, with P being the change of basis matrix.

The matrix P is sometimes called a similarity transformation. In the context of matrix groups, similarity is sometimes referred to as conjugacy, with _____ matrices being conjugate.

  a. Similar
  b. Cartan matrix
  c. Zero matrix
  d. Skew-symmetric

13. A _____ is one of the basic shapes of geometry: a polygon with three corners or vertices and three sides or edges which are line segments. A _____ with vertices A, B, and C is denoted ABC.

In Euclidean geometry any three non-collinear points determine a unique _____ and a unique plane (i.e. a two-dimensional Euclidean space.)

  a. Triangle
  b. 2-bridge knot
  c. -equivalence
  d. -module

14. In mathematics, the _____ of a vector space V is the cardinality (i.e. the number of vectors) of a basis of V. It is sometimes called Hamel _____ or algebraic _____ to distinguish it from other types of _____. All bases of a vector space have equal cardinality and so the _____ of a vector space is uniquely defined. The _____ of the vector space V over the field F can be written as $\dim_F(V)$ or as [V : F], read '_____ of V over F'.

  a. Partial trace
  b. Cofactor
  c. Dual basis
  d. Dimension

Chapter 7. RATIONAL EXPRESSIONS 37

15. The term _____ or centre is used in various contexts in abstract algebra to denote the set of all those elements that commute with all other elements. More specifically:

- The _____ of a group G consists of all those elements x in G such that xg = gx for all g in G. This is a normal subgroup of G.
- The _____ of a ring R is the subset of R consisting of all those elements x of R such that xr = rx for all r in R. The _____ is a commutative subring of R, so R is an algebra over its _____.
- The _____ of an algebra A consists of all those elements x of A such that xa = ax for all a in A. See also: central simple algebra.
- The _____ of a Lie algebra L consists of all those elements x in L such that [x,a] = 0 for all a in L. This is an ideal of the Lie algebra L.
- The _____ of a monoidal category C consists of pairs (A,u) where A is an object of C, and $u: A \otimes - \to - \otimes A$ a natural isomorphism satisfying certain axioms.

a. Self-adjoint
b. Left alternative
c. Ring theory
d. Center

16. In abstract algebra, the _____ of a module is a measure of the module's 'size'. It is defined as the _____ of the longest ascending chain of submodules and is a generalization of the concept of dimension for vector spaces. The modules with finite _____ share many important properties with finite-dimensional vector spaces.

a. Length
b. Supermodule
c. Morita equivalence
d. Finitely generated module

Chapter 8. ROOTS AND RADICALS

1. In mathematics, a _____ of a number x is any number which, when repeatedly multiplied by itself, eventually yields x:

$$r \times r \times \cdots \times r = x.$$

In terms of exponentiation, r is a _____ of x if

$$r^n = x$$

for some positive integer n. For example, 2 is a _____ of 16 since 2^4 = 2 × 2 × 2 × 2 = 16.

The number n is called the degree of the _____.

   a. Rationalisation
   b. Difference of two squares
   c. Cubic function
   d. Root

2. In mathematics, a _____ of a number x is a number r such that r^2 = x, or, in other words, a number r whose square (the result of multiplying the number by itself) is x.

Every non-negative real number x has a unique non-negative _____, called the principal _____, which is denoted with a radical symbol as $\sqrt{x}$, or, using exponent notation, as $x^{1/2}$. For example, the principal _____ of 9 is 3, denoted $\sqrt{9} = 3$, because 3^2 = 3 × 3 = 9.

   a. -module
   b. -equivalence
   c. 2-bridge knot
   d. Square root

3. A _____ is a three-dimensional solid object bounded by six square faces, facets or sides, with three meeting at each vertex. The _____ can also be called a regular hexahedron and is one of the five Platonic solids. It is a special kind of square prism, of rectangular parallelepiped and of trigonal trapezohedron.

   a. equivalence
   b. Cube
   c. 2-bridge knot
   d. -module

Chapter 8. ROOTS AND RADICALS

4. In mathematics, a _____ of a number, denoted $\sqrt[3]{x}$ or $x^{1/3}$, is a number a such that $a^3 = x$. All real numbers have exactly one real _____ and a pair of complex conjugate roots, and all nonzero complex numbers have three distinct complex cube roots. For example, the real _____ of 8 is 2, because $2^3 = 8$.
    a. -module
    b. -equivalence
    c. 2-bridge knot
    d. Cube root

5. In mathematics, specifically group theory, the _____ of a subgroup H in a group G is the e;relative sizee; of H in G. For example, if H has _____ 2 in G, then intuitively e;halfe; of the elements of G lie in H. The _____ of H in G is usually denoted $|G : H|$ or $[G : H]$.

    If G and H are finite groups, then the _____ of H in G is simply the quotient of the orders of the two groups:

    $$|G : H| = \frac{|G|}{|H|}.$$

    By Lagrange's theorem, this number is always a positive integer.

    If G and H are infinite, then the _____ of H is G is defined as the number of cosets of H in G.

    a. Even permutations
    b. Inner automorphism
    c. Outer automorphism
    d. Index

6. The _____ of a Lie algebra $\mathfrak{g}$ is a particular ideal of $\mathfrak{g}$.

    Let $\mathfrak{g}$ be a Lie algebra. The _____ of $\mathfrak{g}$ is defined as the largest solvable ideal of $\mathfrak{g}$.

    a. Garside element
    b. Class sum
    c. Cyclically reduced word
    d. Radical

7. In mathematics, the word _____ is a term for any well-formed combination of mathematical symbols. For example,

$x^2 + 3x - 4$

is an _____, while

)x) / 0

is not, because the parentheses are not balanced and division by zero is undefined.

Being an _____ is a syntactic concept - the meaning of the variables is irrelevant, but different fields have different notions of validity.â€See formal language for how expressions are constructed, and formal semantics for meaning.

a. Orthogonal
b. Unit ring
c. Arity
d. Expression

8. _____ is the mathematical process of putting things together. The plus sign '+' means that numbers are added together. For example, in the picture on the right, there are 3 + 2 apples--meaning three apples and two other apples--which is the same as five apples, since 3 + 2 = 5.

a. Abelian P-root group
b. ADE classification
c. AKS primality test
d. Addition

9. _____ is one of the four basic arithmetic operations; it is the inverse of addition, meaning that if we start with any number and add any number and then subtract the same number we added, we return to the number we started with. _____ is denoted by a minus sign in infix notation.

The traditional names for the parts of the formula

c − b = a

are minuend (c) − subtrahend (b) = difference (a.)

a. 2-bridge knot
b. -equivalence
c. -module
d. Subtraction

10. In mathematics, the complex numbers are an extension of the real numbers obtained by adjoining an imaginary unit, denoted i, which satisfies:

$$i^2 = -1.$$

Every _____ can be written in the form a + bi, where a and b are real numbers called the real part and the imaginary part of the _____, respectively.

Complex numbers are a field, and thus have addition, subtraction, multiplication, and division operations. These operations extend the corresponding operations on real numbers, although with a number of additional elegant and useful properties, e.g., negative real numbers can be obtained by squaring complex (imaginary) numbers.

a. -module
b. -equivalence
c. 2-bridge knot
d. Complex number

11. In mathematics, especially in elementary arithmetic, _____ is an arithmetic operation which is the inverse of multiplication.

Specifically, if c times b equals a, written:

$$c \times b = a$$

where b is not zero, then a divided by b equals c, written:

$$\frac{a}{b} = c$$

For instance,

$$\frac{6}{3} = 2$$

since

$$2 \times 3 = 6.$$

In the above expression, a is called the dividend, b the divisor and c the quotient.

a. -equivalence
b. -module
c. 2-bridge knot
d. Division

12. In algebra, a _____ of an element in a quadratic extension field of a field K is its image under the unique non-identity automorphism of the extended field that fixes K. If the extension is generated by a square root of an element r of K, then the _____ of $a + b\sqrt{r}$ is $a - b\sqrt{r}$ for $a, b \in K$, and in particular in the case of the field C of complex numbers as an extension of the field R of real numbers (where r = − 1), the complex _____ of a + bi is a − bi.

Forming the sum or product of any element of the extension field with its _____ always gives an element of K. This can be used to rewrite a quotient of numbers in the extended field so that the denominator lies in K, by multiplying numerator and denominator by the _____ of the denominator. This process is called rationalization of the denominator, in particular if K is the field Q of rational numbers.

a. Field arithmetic
b. K-theory
c. Digital root
d. Conjugate

13. In mathematics, an _____ represents a solution, such as that to an equation, that emerges from the process of solving the problem but is not a valid solution to the original problem. A missing solution is a solution that was a valid solution to the original problem, but disappeared during the process of solving the problem. Both are frequently the consequence of performing operations that are not invertible for some or all values of the variables, which disturbs the chain of logical implications in the proof.
a. Equating the coefficients
b. Unitary method
c. Extraneous solution
d. Unary operation

14. In mathematics, the _____ of a vector space V is the cardinality (i.e. the number of vectors) of a basis of V. It is sometimes called Hamel _____ or algebraic _____ to distinguish it from other types of _____. All bases of a vector space have equal cardinality and so the _____ of a vector space is uniquely defined. The _____ of the vector space V over the field F can be written as $\dim_F(V)$ or as [V : F], read '_____ of V over F'.

a. Dual basis
b. Dimension
c. Partial trace
d. Cofactor

Chapter 9. SOLVING QUADRATIC EQUATIONS

1. In mathematics, a _____ is a polynomial equation of the second degree. The general form is

$$ax^2 + bx + c = 0$$

The quadratic coefficient a is the coefficient of x^2, the linear coefficient b is the coefficient of x, and c is the constant coefficient, also called the free term or constant term.

Quadratic equations are called quadratic because the variable in the leading term is squared.

   a. Quadratic equation
   b. Difference of two squares
   c. Rationalisation
   d. Cubic function

2. In mathematics, a _____ of a number x is a number r such that r^2 = x, or, in other words, a number r whose square (the result of multiplying the number by itself) is x.

Every non-negative real number x has a unique non-negative _____, called the principal _____, which is denoted with a radical symbol as $\sqrt{x}$, or, using exponent notation, as $x^{1/2}$. For example, the principal _____ of 9 is 3, denoted $\sqrt{9} = 3$, because 3^2 = 3 × 3 = 9.

   a. 2-bridge knot
   b. -module
   c. -equivalence
   d. Square root

3. In elementary algebra, _____ is a technique for converting a quadratic polynomial of the form

$$ax^2 + bx + c$$

to the form

$$a(\cdots\cdots)^2 + \text{constant}.$$

The expression inside the parenthesis is of the form x − constant. Thus one converts ax^2 + bx + c to

$$a(x - h)^2 + k$$

and one must find h and k.

Chapter 9. SOLVING QUADRATIC EQUATIONS

_____ is used in

- solving quadratic equations,
- graphing quadratic functions,
- evaluating integrals in calculus,
- finding Laplace transforms.

In mathematics, _____ is considered a basic algebraic operation, and is often applied without remark in any computation involving quadratic polynomials.

There is a simple formula in elementary algebra for computing the square of a binomial:

$$(x+p)^2 = x^2 + 2px + p^2.$$

For example:

$$(x+3)^2 = x^2 + 6x + 9 \qquad (p=3)$$
$$(x-5)^2 = x^2 - 10x + 25 \qquad (p=-5).$$

In any perfect square, the number p is always half the coefficient of x, and then the constant term is equal to p^2.

a. Content
b. Nested radical
c. Reduct
d. Completing the square

4. In algebra, the _____ is a theorem for finding out the factors of a polynomial (an expression in which the terms are only added, subtracted or multiplied, e.g. x^2 + 6x + 6.) It is a special case of the polynomial remainder theorem.

The _____ states that a polynomial f(x) has a factor x − k if and only if f(k) = 0.

a. Factor theorem
b. Difference polynomial
c. Quadratic function
d. Remez algorithm

5. In mathematics, a _____ of a number x is any number which, when repeatedly multiplied by itself, eventually yields x:

Chapter 9. SOLVING QUADRATIC EQUATIONS

$$r \times r \times \cdots \times r = x.$$

In terms of exponentiation, r is a _____ of x if

$$r^n = x$$

for some positive integer n. For example, 2 is a _____ of 16 since $2^4 = 2 \times 2 \times 2 \times 2 = 16$.

The number n is called the degree of the _____.

   a. Difference of two squares
   b. Cubic function
   c. Rationalisation
   d. Root

6. In elementary algebra, a _____ is a polynomial consisting of three terms; in other words, a _____ is the sum of three monomials. It can be factored using simple steps.

In linguistics, a _____ is a fixed expression which is made from three words; e.g. 'lights, camera, action', 'signed, sealed, delivered'.

   a. Finitary operation
   b. Hall polynomials
   c. Polynomial Diophantine equation
   d. Trinomial

7. In mathematics, the complex numbers are an extension of the real numbers obtained by adjoining an imaginary unit, denoted i, which satisfies:

$$i^2 = -1.$$

Every _____ can be written in the form a + bi, where a and b are real numbers called the real part and the imaginary part of the _____, respectively.

Complex numbers are a field, and thus have addition, subtraction, multiplication, and division operations. These operations extend the corresponding operations on real numbers, although with a number of additional elegant and useful properties, e.g., negative real numbers can be obtained by squaring complex (imaginary) numbers.

a. Complex number
b. 2-bridge knot
c. -equivalence
d. -module

8. In algebra, the _____ of a polynomial with real or complex coefficients is a certain expression in the coefficients of the polynomial which is a symmetric polynomial in the coefficients and gives information on the nature of the roots; in particular, it is equal to zero if and only if the polynomial has a multiple root (i.e. a root with multiplicity greater than one) in the complex numbers. For example, the _____ of the quadratic polynomial

$$ax^2 + bx + c \text{ is } b^2 - 4ac.$$

The _____ of the cubic polynomial

$$ax^3 + bx^2 + cx + d \text{ is } b^2c^2 - 4ac^3 - 4b^3d - 27a^2d^2 + 18abcd.$$

a. Kazhdan-Lusztig polynomials
b. Polynomial remainder theorem
c. Minimal polynomial
d. Discriminant

9. In geometry, a _____ is a straight curve. When geometry is used to model the real world, lines are used to represent straight objects with negligible width and height. Lines are an idealisation of such objects and have no width or height at all and are usually considered to be infinitely long.
a. -equivalence
b. -module
c. 2-bridge knot
d. Line

10. In mathematics, an _____ is a complex number whose squared value is a real number less than or equal to zero. The imaginary unit, denoted by i or j, is an example of an _____. If y is a real number, then iÂ·y is an _____, because:

$$(i \cdot y)^2 = i^2 \cdot y^2 = -y^2 \leq 0.$$

Imaginary numbers were defined in 1572 by Rafael Bombelli.

a. Imaginary Number
b. Abelian P-root group
c. AKS primality test
d. ADE classification

11. In mathematics, a _____ in a (unital) ring R is an invertible element of R, i.e. an element u such that there is a v in R with

uv = vu = 1_R, where 1_R is the multiplicative identity element.

That is, u is an invertible element of the multiplicative monoid of R. If $0 \neq 1$ in the ring, then 0 is not a _____.

Unfortunately, the term _____ is also used to refer to the identity element 1_R of the ring, in expressions like ring with a _____ or _____ ring, and also e.g. '_____' matrix.

a. Ore condition
b. Ascending chain condition on principal ideals
c. Ore extension
d. Unit

12. _____ is the mathematical process of putting things together. The plus sign '+' means that numbers are added together. For example, in the picture on the right, there are 3 + 2 apples--meaning three apples and two other apples--which is the same as five apples, since 3 + 2 = 5.

a. Abelian P-root group
b. ADE classification
c. Addition
d. AKS primality test

13. _____ is one of the four basic arithmetic operations; it is the inverse of addition, meaning that if we start with any number and add any number and then subtract the same number we added, we return to the number we started with. _____ is denoted by a minus sign in infix notation.

The traditional names for the parts of the formula

c − b = a

are minuend (c) − subtrahend (b) = difference (a.)

a. 2-bridge knot
b. -module
c. -equivalence
d. Subtraction

14. In mathematics, the (formal) _____ of a complex vector space V is the complex vector space $\overline{V}$ consisting of all formal complex conjugates of elements of V. That is, $\overline{V}$ is a vector space whose elements are in one-to-one correspondence with the elements of V:

$$\overline{V} = \{\overline{v} \mid v \in V\},$$

with the following rules for addition and scalar multiplication:

$$\overline{v} + \overline{w} = \overline{v + w} \quad \text{and} \quad \alpha \overline{v} = \overline{\overline{\alpha} v}.$$

Here v and w are vectors in V, α is a complex number, and $\overline{\alpha}$ denotes the _____ of α.

In the case where V is a linear subspace of $\mathbb{C}^n$, the formal _____ $\overline{V}$ is naturally isomorphic to the actual _____ subspace of V in $\mathbb{C}^n$.

a. Binomial inverse theorem
b. Conjugate transpose
c. Polynomial basis
d. Complex conjugate

15. In algebra, a _____ of an element in a quadratic extension field of a field K is its image under the unique non-identity automorphism of the extended field that fixes K. If the extension is generated by a square root of an element r of K, then the _____ of $a + b\sqrt{r}$ is $a - b\sqrt{r}$ for $a, b \in K$, and in particular in the case of the field C of complex numbers as an extension of the field R of real numbers (where r = − 1), the complex _____ of a + bi is a − bi.

Forming the sum or product of any element of the extension field with its _____ always gives an element of K. This can be used to rewrite a quotient of numbers in the extended field so that the denominator lies in K, by multiplying numerator and denominator by the _____ of the denominator. This process is called rationalization of the denominator, in particular if K is the field Q of rational numbers.

a. Digital root
b. K-theory
c. Field arithmetic
d. Conjugate

16. In mathematics, especially in elementary arithmetic, _____ is an arithmetic operation which is the inverse of multiplication.

Specifically, if c times b equals a, written:

$$c \times b = a$$

where b is not zero, then a divided by b equals c, written:

$$\frac{a}{b} = c$$

For instance,

$$\frac{6}{3} = 2$$

since

$$2 \times 3 = 6.$$

In the above expression, a is called the dividend, b the divisor and c the quotient.

a. -equivalence
b. Division
c. 2-bridge knot
d. -module

17. In mathematics, the _____ is a conic section, the intersection of a right circular conical surface and a plane parallel to a generating straight line of that surface. Given a point (the focus) and a line (the directrix) that lie in a plane, the locus of points in that plane that are equidistant to them is a _____.

A particular case arises when the plane is tangent to the conical surface of a circle.

Chapter 9. SOLVING QUADRATIC EQUATIONS

a. -equivalence
b. Parabola
c. -module
d. 2-bridge knot

18. The set of all symmetry operations considered, on all objects in a set X, can be modeled as a group action g : G × X → X, where the image of g in G and x in X is written as gÂ·x. If, for some g, gÂ·x = y then x and y are said to be symmetrical to each other. For each object x, operations g for which gÂ·x = x form a group, the _____ of the object, a subgroup of G. If the _____ of x is the trivial group then x is said to be asymmetric, otherwise symmetric.

a. 2-bridge knot
b. -module
c. Symmetry group
d. -equivalence

19. In mathematics, a _____ in a topological space X is a continuous map f from the unit interval I = [0,1] to X

$f : I \to X.$

The initial point of the _____ is f(0) and the terminal point is f(1.) One often speaks of a '_____ from x to y' where x and y are the initial and terminal points of the _____.

a. Simplicial complex
b. Suspension
c. Genus
d. Path

Chapter 1
1. d   2. c   3. d   4. d   5. a   6. c   7. a   8. d   9. d   10. d
11. d   12. d   13. c   14. c   15. d   16. d   17. d   18. c   19. b   20. c
21. d   22. d

Chapter 2
1. a   2. d   3. a   4. d   5. c   6. d   7. d   8. d   9. d   10. b
11. d

Chapter 3
1. c   2. d   3. b   4. d   5. a   6. c   7. a   8. d

Chapter 4
1. d   2. d   3. d   4. b   5. d   6. c   7. a   8. a

Chapter 5
1. d   2. d   3. d   4. b   5. c   6. d   7. d   8. d   9. c   10. a
11. d   12. c

Chapter 6
1. b   2. d   3. d   4. d   5. b   6. d   7. d   8. d   9. d   10. b
11. d   12. a   13. d   14. d   15. d   16. b   17. b   18. c   19. a   20. b
21. d

Chapter 7
1. d   2. a   3. d   4. b   5. d   6. d   7. d   8. b   9. d   10. d
11. a   12. a   13. a   14. d   15. d   16. a

Chapter 8
1. d   2. d   3. b   4. d   5. d   6. d   7. d   8. d   9. d   10. d
11. d   12. d   13. c   14. b

Chapter 9
1. a   2. d   3. d   4. a   5. d   6. d   7. a   8. d   9. d   10. a
11. d   12. c   13. d   14. d   15. d   16. b   17. b   18. c   19. d